Spices

a cook's guide to spicy recipes

This is a Parragon Publishing book
This edition published in 2006

Parragon Publishing
Queen Street House
4 Queen Street
Bath BA1 1HE, UK

Copyright © Parragon Books Ltd 2006

ISBN-1-40547-165-4

Printed in Malaysia
Designed by Shelley Doyle at 20 Twenty Design

This book uses imperial, metric, and US cup measurements. Follow the same units of
measurement throughout; do not mix metric and imperial. All spoon measurements are
level, unless otherwise stated: teaspoons are assumed to be 5ml and tablespoons are
assumed to be 15ml. Unless otherwise stated, milk is assumed to be whole, eggs and
individual fruits such as bananas are medium, and pepper is freshly ground black pepper.

Recipes using raw or very lightly cooked eggs should be avoided by infants, the elderly,
pregnant women, convalescents and anyone suffering from an illness. Pregnant and
breast-feeding women are advised to avoid eating peanuts and peanut products.

CONTENTS

INTRODUCTION

The roots, stems, seeds, berries, buds, pods, and bark of a huge number of different plants, native to many different countries across the world, are the source of spices, but the one thing they have in common is that they are all highly aromatic. They have been valued for the fragrances and flavors they impart to both savory and sweet dishes in a vast range of world-wide cuisines. Indeed, they were regarded as so precious that wars have been fought, explorers have died, taxes have been raised, and empires have been created in the search for these invaluable commodities.

If this seems like overstating the case, just think of those perennial favorites we would have to do without if the spice routes had never been opened—from onion bhajias to cinnamon rolls and from pulao rice to chicken satay. Whether your tastes lie with fiery chili, pungent cumin, warming cinnamon, sharp ginger, sweet coriander, or subtle saffron, spices add depth and range to all kinds of dishes and often also bring out the flavors of other ingredients. The dinner table would be a very bland and boring place without them.

WHICH SPICE?

There are no hard-and-fast rules about which spices to use with particular ingredients, although there are many traditional combinations. For example, green peppercorns often partner duck, saffron features in classic rice dishes from Iran to Italy, and ginger has a natural affinity with chilies in savory dishes and chocolate in sweet ones. Curries, in all their many forms and nationalities, are invariably based on a balanced mixture of spices. As many as ten carefully blended spices is not at all unusual, whether the main ingredient is chicken, vegetables, or fish. As with all cooking, it's worth experimenting to discover new flavors and original ways of using the spices that you like best. For example, custard tart is usually livened up with grated nutmeg, but there is no reason why you shouldn't try adding ground cardamom instead.

Many people associate the word spicy with hot food and certainly there are a number of warming spices, such as cinnamon, ginger, paprika, and cumin. All forms of chilies—fresh and dried, chili powder and cayenne pepper—are hot and some are really fiery. However, many other popular spices are aromatic rather than hot giving foods an almost perfumed flavor. If you don't like hotly spiced food, don't simply dismiss all spices out of hand and overlook such delicious flavorings as coriander seeds, cardamom, and saffron.

Some spices, such as cloves, are very strongly flavored and should always be used sparingly. Others are more delicate and subtle and can be used in larger amounts if they appeal to your taste. The best guide is to follow the recipe instructions the first time you try a new flavor and, if you like it, you can increase the quantity the next time you make the dish. However, spices should always be used to enhance the flavors of other ingredients, not to suppress them entirely.

BUYING AND STORING SPICES

Most spices are, by definition, dried; there are only a few exceptions, the most common being fresh gingerroot. Their fragrance and flavor comes from highly volatile essential oils which are easily destroyed by exposure to air, humidity, sunlight, and other high risk factors common in the average kitchen. Consequently, it is best to buy spices in small quantities, unless there are one or two particular ones that you know you will use almost every day, such as black pepper. Whole spices stay fresher for longer than ready ground ones but, as a general rule, all types lose much of their flavor, aroma, and color once they have been stored for about six months. In any case, keep an eye on the "use-by" date on the original packaging.

Whether whole or ground, spices are best stored in airtight glass containers. You can keep the jars in a cool, dark cupboard or use tinted glass containers stored on a rack away from the oven, stovetop or a radiator. Fresh gingerroot may be stored in the refrigerator (see page 7) and its close cousins, galangal and fresh turmeric, can be stored in the same way.

USING SPICES

The aromatic oils that give spices their unique aroma and flavor evaporate very fast so it is often better to use whole spices and grind or grate them immediately before use, rather than use ready ground ones. Seeds, such as cumin and coriander, are easy to grind in a mortar with a pestle, in a spice grinder, or even a coffee grinder kept specifically for the purpose. Nutmeg is always most flavorsome if the seed is freshly grated.

Dry-frying or toasting is a good way to bring out the flavor of some spices. Heat a heavy skillet without any oil or other fat. Add the seeds and cook over medium heat, tossing and stirring frequently, for a few minutes until they give off their aroma and start to pop. Tip into a grinder or mortar and then crush before adding to the other ingredients.

Spices that are used whole, such as cinnamon sticks, should be removed from the dish before serving.

FAVORITE SPICES

This is a guide to the most commonly used spices and the ones which appear most frequently in the recipes in this book. However, it is by no means exhaustive. Store the spices as described on page 5, unless otherwise stated.

ALLSPICE: These small berries are so named because they taste like a mixture of cinnamon, nutmeg, and cloves with a hint of ginger. They may be used whole or ground in sweet and savory dishes, as well as in pickles.

NUTMEG: This large brown seed from a tropical evergreen tree has a sweet, nutty flavor that works well in both savory and sweet dishes. It is an essential ingredient in béchamel sauce and is frequently used to flavor cakes, pies, and desserts, especially milk puddings. It features in the cuisines of countries across the world. It is best used freshly grated, but ground nutmeg is also available.

CLOVES: These little dried flower buds, originating from Southeast Asia, are a familiar sight in Western kitchens where they are used to stud onions, baked cured ham, and apples and for flavoring mulled wine. Ground cloves are widely used in baking, imparting a strong, aromatic flavor.

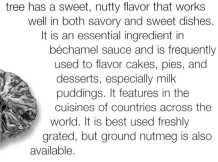

CARDAMOM: An expensive spice that is highly valued in the cuisines of northern Europe, India, the Middle East, and North Africa, cardamom pods may be pale green, beige, or dark brown. The first two have the best flavor for both savory and sweet dishes and are used in coffee in the Middle East and tea in India. To grind, remove the seeds from the pod and rub them between your fingers to separate first. The seeds may also be used whole.

PEPPERCORNS: White, black, and green peppercorns are all fruit of the same plant picked at different stages of ripeness. They range from fragrant to pungent and may be used whole or ground to bring out the flavor of other ingredients as well as adding their own distinctive flavor. Pepper is used most often in savory dishes, but has a surprisingly good effect in sweet dishes, such as sprinkled over strawberries.

CORIANDER: The small, ridged, brown seeds of the cilantro plant are available whole or ready ground. The sweet, delicate spicy flavor is suited to both sweet and savory dishes and coriander is an essential ingredient in curry powder. It features in Indian, Southeast Asian, and Moroccan cooking and is widely used in pickling.

CUMIN: Truly the flavor of the Middle East and North Africa, these small, ridged, light brown seeds have a distinctive warm and pungent flavor. Cumin is also an essential ingredient of garam masala (see opposite). It is available whole or ground and is often lightly toasted before use.

TURMERIC: This resembles gingerroot in appearance and belongs to the same family. It is usually sold ground into a yellow powder, which can stain your hands. It is widely used in Indian and Middle Eastern cuisine and in many pickles, providing a rich golden color. It has a slightly bitter taste and should be used sparingly.

SAFFRON: The world's most expensive spice, this is obtained from the stigmas of a flowering crocus and the finest saffron, said to come from La Mancha in Spain, is harvested by hand. Its inimitable slightly bitter flavor and delicate fragrance—superb with rice dishes—are highly valued in the cooking of Spain, North Africa, India, Kashmir, Egypt, and Iran. It also provides the characteristic flavor and golden color of some traditional baked recipes, such as saffron bread. It is better to buy saffron threads rather than the less expensive powder. To use, simply steep them in a little liquid, such as stock, before adding to the other ingredients.

GINGER: This Asian root was one of the earliest spices known to Western cooks and features in both savory and sweet dishes. It is widely used in Chinese, Southeast Asian, and Indian cuisines. The fresh root has the strongest flavor and most pungent, almost sweet aroma. Choose smooth, plump roots. Thinly peel the skin with a swivel blade vegetable peeler and slice, chop, or grate the flesh according to the recipe. Tightly wrapped, unpeeled roots may be stored in the refrigerator for up to six weeks. Ground ginger is used extensively in baking, especially cakes and cookies, but is not an adequate substitute when fresh gingerroot is specified. However, fresh ginger may be substituted for ground. Ginger is also available preserved in syrup and candied.

CINNAMON: Made from the dried bark of an Indian evergreen tree, this warm, fragrant, versatile spice is available rolled into sticks—most often used in savory dishes and poached fruit—and ground—the easiest choice for cakes and cookies. It is difficult to grind the sticks at home. Cinnamon is widely used in Middle Eastern dishes and is excellent for spiced drinks.

CURRY POWDER: This is not traditionally used in India. Many commercial brands are available or you can make your own by grinding a mixture of cumin seeds, fennel seeds, coriander seeds, dried chilies, fenugreek seeds, and curry leaves and then mixing it with chili powder, ground turmeric, and salt in proportions to suit your taste.

GARAM MASALA: This mixture of, literally "hot spices" is usually added by Indian cooks toward the end of the cooking time or sprinkled over dishes as a garnish. Most Indian cooks have their own recipes that will usually include mustard seeds, cumin seeds, coriander seeds, fenugreek seeds, black peppercorns, cinnamon, curry leaves, and dried chilies. They are usually roasted before grinding and combining.

CHILI POWDER: It is easy to make your own version by grinding or crushing dried chilies, with or without the seeds according to taste. Commercial brands vary both in heat and in purity as cheaper versions may include other spices and artificial coloring.

PAPRIKA: Widely used in Hungarian, Austrian, Spanish, and Middle Eastern dishes, this is a mixture of ground, dried red peppers. It may be mild, often labeled sweet, or hot but it is never so fiery as chili powder.

APPETIZERS

Sizzling appetizers that will set the taste buds tingling are sure to stimulate the appetite. Spicy treats, from Tex-Mex ribs to Thai vegetable fritters with a chili dipping sauce make a lively start to any meal, while delicious, warming soups provide a perfect welcome to hungry guests on a cold evening.

INGREDIENTS

4 cups water

generous 1¼ cups toor dal or chana dal

1 tsp paprika

½ tsp chili powder

½ tsp ground turmeric

2 tbsp ghee or vegetable oil

1 fresh green chili, seeded and
finely chopped

1 tsp cumin seeds

3 curry leaves, coarsely torn

1 tsp sugar

salt

1 tsp garam masala,
to garnish

PREPARE 5 MINUTES

COOK 40 MINUTES

SERVES 4

Bring the water to a boil in a large, heavy-bottom pan. Add the dal, cover, and let simmer, stirring occasionally, for 25 minutes.

Stir in the paprika, chili powder, and turmeric, re-cover and cook for an additional 10 minutes, or until the dal is tender.

Meanwhile, heat the ghee in a small skillet. Add the chili, cumin seeds, and curry leaves and cook, stirring constantly, for 1 minute.

Add the spice mixture to the dal. Stir in the sugar and season with salt to taste. Ladle into warmed soup bowls, sprinkle with garam masala, and serve immediately.

Lentil Soup

Spinach Soup

INGREDIENTS

2 tsp coriander seeds

2 tsp cumin seeds

1 tbsp ghee or vegetable oil

2 onions, chopped

1 tbsp ginger paste

2 tsp garlic paste

6 curry leaves, coarsely torn

2 dried red chilies, crushed

2 tsp black mustard seeds

½ tsp fenugreek seeds

1 tsp ground turmeric

1 cup masoor dal

2 potatoes, diced

5 cups vegetable stock

2 lb 4 oz/1 kg fresh spinach, tough stalks removed, plus extra to garnish

2 tbsp lemon juice

1¼ cups coconut milk

salt and pepper

Heat a heavy-bottom skillet and dry-fry the coriander and cumin seeds, stirring constantly, until they give off their aroma. Tip into a mortar and grind with a pestle. Alternatively, grind in a spice mill or blender.

Heat the ghee in a large pan. Add the onions, ginger paste, garlic paste, curry leaves, chilies, mustard seeds, and fenugreek seeds and cook over low heat, stirring frequently, for 8 minutes, or until the onions are softened and golden. Stir in the ground, dry-fried spices and turmeric and cook for an additional 1 minute. Add the masoor dal, potatoes, and stock and bring to a boil, then reduce the heat and let simmer for 15 minutes, or until the potatoes are tender. Stir in the spinach and cook for an additional 2–3 minutes, or until wilted.

Remove the pan from the heat and let cool slightly. Ladle the soup into a food processor or blender and process until smooth. Return to the pan and stir in the lemon juice and coconut milk and season to taste with salt and pepper. Reheat gently, stirring occasionally, but do not boil. Ladle into warmed soup bowls, garnish with fresh spinach leaves, and serve immediately.

2 lb/900 g chicken breast meat,
cut into ¼-inch/5-mm thick,
1-inch/2.5-cm wide strips

MARINADE

1 lemongrass stem (tender inner part only)

2 tbsp vegetable oil

2 tbsp soy sauce

2 tsp tamarind paste

2 garlic cloves, crushed

1 tsp ground cumin

1 tsp ground coriander

1 tbsp lime juice

1 tsp brown sugar

PEANUT SAUCE

2 tbsp smooth peanut butter

generous ¾ cup coconut cream

2 tsp Thai red curry paste

1 tbsp fish sauce

1 tbsp brown sugar

PREPARE 15 MINUTES,
PLUS 1 HOUR MARINATING

COOK 15 MINUTES

SERVES 8

Thread the chicken on to presoaked bamboo skewers.

To make the marinade, chop the lemongrass and place in a food processor with the oil, soy sauce, tamarind paste, garlic, cumin, coriander, lime juice, and sugar. Process to a paste. Transfer to a bowl.

Add the chicken to the marinade and toss to coat. Cover with plastic wrap and let marinate in the refrigerator for at least 1 hour.

Preheat the broiler to medium. Place the peanut butter, coconut cream, red curry paste, fish sauce, and sugar in a pan. Heat gently, stirring constantly, to form a smooth sauce.

Cook the chicken under the hot broiler for 3–5 minutes on each side, or until the chicken is cooked through. Alternatively, grill over medium–hot coals. Reheat the sauce, adding a little hot water if necessary, and serve with the chicken satay.

Chicken Satay

Pork Tostadas

PREPARE 15 MINUTES

COOK 30 MINUTES

SERVES 6–8

INGREDIENTS

1 tbsp vegetable oil, plus extra
for the tortillas

1 small onion, finely chopped

2 garlic cloves, finely chopped

1 lb/450 g freshly ground pork

2 tsp ground cumin

2 tsp chili powder, plus extra to garnish

1 tsp ground cinnamon

salt and pepper

6 soft corn tortillas, cut into wedges

TO SERVE

shredded iceberg lettuce

sour cream

red bell pepper, cored, seeded,
and finely diced

tomato salsa (optional)

Heat 1 tablespoon of oil in a heavy-bottom skillet over medium heat. Add the onion and garlic and cook, stirring frequently, for 5 minutes, or until softened. Increase the heat, add the ground pork, and cook, stirring constantly to break up any lumps, until well browned.

Add the cumin, chili powder, cinnamon, and salt and pepper to taste and cook, stirring, for 2 minutes. Cover and cook over low heat, stirring occasionally, for 10 minutes.

Meanwhile, heat a little oil in a nonstick skillet. Add the tortilla wedges, in batches, and cook on both sides until crisp. Drain on paper towels. Transfer the wedges to a serving plate and top with the pork mixture, followed by the lettuce, a little sour cream, and some bell pepper. Garnish with a sprinkling of chili powder and serve at once with a little tomato salsa for extra flavor, if desired.

INGREDIENTS

2 racks of pork ribs,
about 1 lb 7 oz/650 g each

vegetable oil, for brushing

TENNESSEE RUB

1 tbsp ground cumin

1 tsp garlic salt

½ tsp ground cinnamon

½ tsp dry English mustard powder

½ tsp ground coriander

1 tsp dried mixed herbs

pinch of cayenne pepper, or to taste

BOURBON BARBECUE SAUCE

1 tbsp corn or peanut oil

½ onion, finely chopped

2 large garlic cloves, minced

generous ⅓ cup brown sugar

1 tbsp dry English mustard powder

1 tsp ground cumin

2 tbsp tomato paste

6 tbsp bourbon

2 tbsp Worcestershire sauce

2 tbsp apple or white wine vinegar

few drops of hot pepper sauce, to taste

**PREPARE 15 MINUTES,
PLUS 8 HOURS' MARINATING**

COOK 1½–2 HOURS

SERVES 4–6

A day ahead, mix all the ingredients for the rub together in a small bowl. Rub the mixture onto both sides of the ribs, then cover and let marinate in the refrigerator overnight.

To make the Barbecue Sauce, heat the oil in a pan over medium-high heat. Add the onion and garlic and cook for 5 minutes, stirring frequently, or until the onion is soft. Stir in the remaining sauce ingredients. Slowly bring to a boil, stirring to dissolve the sugar, then reduce the heat and let simmer, uncovered, for 30 minutes–1 hour, stirring occasionally, until dark brown and very thick. Let cool, then cover and let chill until required.

When ready to barbecue, heat the coals until they are glowing. Brush the barbecue rack with a little oil. Put the ribs onto the rack and cook, turning frequently, for 40 minutes, or until the meat feels tender. If they appear to be drying out, brush with water.

Remove the ribs from the barbecue and, when cool enough to handle, cut them into 1- or ½-rib portions. Return the rib portions to the barbecue and brush with the sauce. Cook the ribs, turning frequently and basting generously with the sauce, for an additional 10 minutes, or until they are dark brown and glossy. Serve with any remaining sauce, reheated, to use for dipping— and plenty of paper napkins for sticky fingers!

Barbecue Rack of Ribs

Miniature Pork Brochettes

PREPARE 15 MINUTES,
PLUS 8 HOURS' MARINATING

COOK 15 MINUTES

MAKES 12

INGREDIENTS

1 lb/450 g lean, boneless pork

3 tbsp Spanish olive oil, plus extra for
oiling (optional)

grated rind and juice of
1 large lemon

2 garlic cloves, crushed

2 tbsp chopped fresh flatleaf parsley, plus
extra to garnish

1 tbsp ras-el-hanout spice blend

salt and pepper

The brochettes are marinated overnight, so remember to do this in advance in order that they are ready when you need them. Cut the pork into pieces about 3/4 inch/2 cm square and put in a large, shallow, nonmetallic dish that will hold the pieces in a single layer.

To prepare the marinade, place all the remaining ingredients in a bowl and mix together. Pour the marinade over the pork and toss the meat in it until well coated. Cover the dish and let marinate in the refrigerator for 8 hours or overnight, stirring the pork 2–3 times.

You can use wooden or metal skewers to cook the brochettes and for this recipe you will need about 12 x 6-inch/15-cm skewers. If you are using wooden ones, soak them in cold water for 30 minutes prior to using. This helps to stop them burning and the food sticking to them during cooking. Metal skewers simply need to be greased, and flat ones should be used in preference to round ones to prevent the food on them falling off.

Preheat the broiler, grill pan, or grill. Thread 3 marinated pork pieces, leaving a little space between each piece, onto each prepared skewer. Cook the brochettes for 10–15 minutes, or until tender and lightly charred, turning several times and basting with the remaining marinade during cooking. Serve the pork brochettes piping hot, garnished with parsley.

1½ tbsp salt

1 lemon, sliced

1 lb 12 oz/800 g large unshelled raw shrimp

REMOULADE SAUCE

2 oz/55 g scallions, coarsely chopped

2 oz/55 g celery stalks, coarsely chopped

1 large garlic clove

4 tbsp chopped fresh parsley

2 tbsp Creole mustard or German mustard

2 tbsp superfine sugar

2 tbsp cider vinegar or tomato ketchup

1½ tbsp prepared horseradish

1 tbsp paprika

½ tsp cayenne pepper

½ tsp salt

¼ tsp ground black pepper

few drops of hot pepper sauce, to taste

about ⅔ cup corn or peanut oil

TO SERVE

shredded iceberg lettuce

2 hard-cooked eggs, shelled and sliced

2 tomatoes, sliced

PREPARE 15 MINUTES, PLUS 45 MINUTES' CHILLING

COOK 5–8 MINUTES

SERVES 4–6

To make the sauce, put the scallions, celery, garlic, and parsley into a food processor and pulse until finely chopped. Add the mustard, sugar, vinegar, horseradish, paprika, cayenne pepper, salt, pepper, and hot pepper sauce to taste and whiz until well blended. With the motor running, slowly pour in the oil through the feed tube in a slow, steady stream until a thick, creamy sauce forms. Transfer to a large bowl, cover, and set aside.

To poach the shrimp, bring a large pan of water with the salt and lemon slices to a boil over high heat. Add the shrimp and cook just until they turn pink.

Drain the shrimp well and put them under cold running water until completely chilled. Shell and devein them, adding them to the sauce as you go. Stir together, then cover and let chill for at least 45 minutes, but ideally overnight. Serve on a bed of lettuce with hard-cooked eggs and sliced tomatoes.

Shrimp Remoulade

Onion Bhajias

INGREDIENTS

½ tsp onion seeds

½ tsp cumin seeds

½ tsp fennel seeds

½ tsp kalonji seeds

1½ cups gram flour

1 tsp baking powder

1 tsp ground turmeric

½ tsp chili powder

pinch of asafoetida

salt

3 onions, thinly sliced

2 fresh green chilies, seeded and finely chopped

3 tbsp chopped fresh cilantro

vegetable oil, for deep-frying

Heat a large, heavy-bottom skillet and dry-fry the onion, cumin, fennel, and kalonji seeds for a few seconds, stirring constantly, until they give off their aroma. Remove from the heat and tip into a mortar. Crush lightly with a pestle and tip into a large bowl.

Sift the flour, baking powder, turmeric, chili powder, asafoetida, and a pinch of salt into the bowl and add the onions, chilies, and chopped cilantro. Mix thoroughly, then gradually stir in enough cold water to make a thick batter.

Heat the vegetable oil in a deep-fat fryer or large, heavy-bottom pan to 350–375°F/180–190°C, or until a cube of bread browns in 30 seconds. Drop spoonfuls of the batter into the hot oil and cook until golden brown, turning once. Remove with a slotted spoon and drain on paper towels. Serve hot.

INGREDIENTS

1 cup all-purpose flour

1 tsp ground coriander

1 tsp ground cumin

1 tsp ground turmeric

1 tsp salt

½ tsp pepper

2 garlic cloves, finely chopped

1¼-inch/3-cm piece fresh gingerroot, chopped

2 small fresh green chilies, finely chopped

1 tbsp chopped cilantro

scant 1 cup cold water

1 onion, chopped

1 potato, coarsely grated

¾ cup canned corn kernels

1 small eggplant, diced

4½ oz/125 g Chinese broccoli, cut into short lengths

coconut oil, for deep-frying

SWEET CHILI DIP

2 fresh red Thai chilies, finely chopped

4 tbsp superfine sugar

4 tbsp rice vinegar or white wine vinegar

1 tbsp light soy sauce

PREPARE 25 MINUTES

COOK 15 MINUTES

SERVES 4

Make the dip by mixing all the ingredients together thoroughly until the sugar is dissolved. Cover and reserve until required.

To make the fritters, place the flour in a bowl and stir in the coriander, cumin, turmeric, salt, and pepper. Add the garlic, ginger, green chilies, and cilantro with just enough of the water to form a thick batter.

Add the onion, potato, corn kernels, eggplant, and broccoli to the batter and stir well to distribute the ingredients evenly.

Heat the oil in a deep skillet or wok to 350–375°F/180–190°C, or until a cube of bread browns in 30 seconds. Drop tablespoons of the batter into the hot oil and cook in batches until golden and crisp, turning once.

Drain the fritters well on paper towels and serve hot with the sweet chili dip.

Vegetable Fritters with Sweet Chili Dip

Soft Dumplings in Yogurt with Masala

INGREDIENTS

1 cup urid dal powder

1 tsp baking powder

½ tsp ground ginger

3 cups water

vegetable oil, for deep-frying

1¾ cups plain yogurt

generous ⅓ cup sugar

sliced fresh red chilies, to garnish

MASALA

1¾ oz/50 g coriander seeds

1¾ oz/50 g white cumin seeds

1 oz/25 g crushed red chilies

3½ oz/100 g citric acid

Place the powdered urid dal in a large bowl. Add the baking powder and ground ginger and stir to mix well. Add $1^1/_4$ cups of the water and mix to form a paste.

Heat the vegetable oil in a deep-fat fryer or large, heavy-bottom pan to 350–375°F/180–190°C, or until a cube of bread browns in 30 seconds. Add the batter, 1 teaspoon at a time, and deep-fry the dumplings until golden brown, lowering the heat when the oil gets too hot. Remove the dumplings with a slotted spoon and set aside.

Place the yogurt in a separate bowl. Add the remaining water and the sugar and mix together with a whisk or fork. Set aside.

To make the masala, roast the coriander and white cumin seeds in a small pan until a little darker in color. Transfer to a food processor and process until coarsely ground. Alternatively, use a mortar and pestle. Add the crushed red chilies and citric acid and blend well together.

Sprinkle 1 tablespoon of the masala over the dumplings and garnish with chopped red chilies. Serve with the reserved yogurt mixture.

MAIN COURSES

Inexpensive, everyday ingredients and easy-to-make dishes become something really special with the addition of well-chosen spices. Tantalizingly fragrant or vibrantly hot meat, chicken, fish, and vegetable main courses—from Tequila Marinated Beef Steaks (see page 38) to Vegetable Korma (see page 50)—are sure to delight family and friends alike.

MAIN COURSES

1¼-inch/3-cm piece fresh gingerroot, finely chopped

2 garlic cloves, finely chopped

1 small onion, finely chopped

1 lemongrass stem, finely chopped

½ tsp salt

1 tsp black peppercorns

3 lb 5 oz/1.5 kg roasting chicken

1 tbsp coconut cream

2 tbsp lime juice

2 tbsp clear honey

1 tsp cornstarch

2 tsp water

stir-fried vegetables, to serve

PREPARE 15 MINUTES, PLUS 8 HOURS' CHILLING

COOK 1 HOUR 20 MINUTES

SERVES 4

Place the ginger, garlic, onion, lemongrass, salt, and peppercorns in a mortar and, using a pestle, grind to a smooth paste.

Using poultry shears or strong kitchen scissors, cut the chicken in half lengthwise. Spread the paste all over the chicken, both inside and out, and spread it on to the flesh under the breast skin. Cover and let chill in the refrigerator for at least several hours or overnight.

Preheat the oven to 350°F/180°C. Heat the coconut cream, lime juice, and honey together in a small pan, stirring until smooth. Brush a little of the mixture evenly over the chicken.

Place the chicken halves on a baking sheet over a roasting pan half filled with boiling water. Roast in the preheated oven for 1 hour, or until the chicken is a rich golden brown color, basting occasionally with the lime and honey mixture.

When the chicken is cooked, boil the water from the roasting pan to reduce it to a scant ½ cup. Blend the cornstarch and water together and stir into the reduced liquid. Bring gently to a boil, then stir until slightly thickened and clear. Serve the chicken with the sauce and freshly cooked stir-fried vegetables.

Roast Chicken with Ginger & Lime

Butter Chicken

PREPARE 15 MINUTES,
PLUS 8 HOURS' MARINATING

COOK 25 MINUTES

SERVES 6

INGREDIENTS

⅔ cup plain yogurt

1 tsp ginger paste

salt

6 skinless, boneless chicken breasts

2 oz/55 g butter

1 cinnamon stick

6 cardamom pods

6 cloves

2 bay leaves

⅔ cup sour cream

⅔ cup light cream

large pinch of saffron threads, crushed

1 tbsp ground almonds

¼ tsp cornstarch

Mix the yogurt, ginger paste, and 1 teaspoon of salt in a large, shallow dish. Cut each chicken breast into 3 pieces and add to the dish. Rub the yogurt mixture into the chicken, then cover with plastic wrap and let marinate in the refrigerator overnight.

Remove the chicken from the dish, reserving any marinade. Melt the butter in a large, heavy-bottom pan, add the chicken, and cook over a low heat, turning occasionally, for 10 minutes, or until browned and nearly cooked through. Remove with a slotted spoon and set aside.

Add the cinnamon, cardamoms, cloves, and bay leaves to the pan and cook, stirring constantly, for 1 minute, or until they give off their aroma. Add the reserved marinade, sour cream, light cream, and saffron, stir well, cover, and let simmer for 5 minutes.

Return the chicken pieces to the pan and stir in the ground almonds. Mix the cornstarch with enough water to make a smooth paste and stir into the pan. Cover and let simmer for 5 minutes, or until the chicken is tender and cooked through. Taste and add more salt, if necessary, and serve immediately.

INGREDIENTS

1 lb/450 g lean boneless pork, cut into 1-inch/2½-cm cubes

all-purpose flour, well seasoned with salt and pepper, for coating

1 tbsp vegetable oil

8 oz/225 g chorizo sausage, outer casing removed, cut into bite-size chunks

1 onion, coarsely chopped

4 garlic cloves, finely chopped

2 celery stalks, chopped

1 cinnamon stick, broken

2 bay leaves

2 tsp allspice

2 carrots, sliced

2–3 fresh red chilies, seeded and finely chopped

6 ripe tomatoes, peeled and chopped

4 cups pork or vegetable stock

2 sweet potatoes, cut into chunks

corn kernels, cut from 1 ear fresh corn

1 tbsp chopped fresh oregano, plus extra oregano sprigs to garnish

salt and pepper

cooked long-grain rice, to serve

PREPARE 25 MINUTES

COOK 2 HOURS

SERVES 4–6

Toss the pork in the seasoned flour to coat. Heat the oil in a large, heavy-bottom pan or ovenproof casserole. Add the chorizo and lightly brown on all sides. Remove the chorizo with a slotted spoon and set aside.

Add the pork, in batches, and cook until browned on all sides. Remove the pork with a slotted spoon and set aside. Add the onion, garlic, and celery to the pan and cook for 5 minutes, or until softened.

Add the cinnamon, bay leaves, and allspice and cook, stirring, for 2 minutes. Add the pork, carrots, chilies, tomatoes, and stock. Bring to a boil, then reduce the heat, cover, and let simmer for 1 hour, or until the pork is tender.

Return the chorizo to the pan with the sweet potatoes, corn, oregano, and salt and pepper to taste. Cover and let simmer for an additional 30 minutes, or until the vegetables are tender. Discard the bay leaves. Serve garnished with oregano sprigs, and with some plain boiled long-grain rice to absorb some of the sauce.

Spicy Pork & Vegetable Stew

Tequila-Marinated Beef Steaks

PREPARE 10 MINUTES,
PLUS 2 HOURS' MARINATING
AND 30 MINUTES' STANDING

COOK 6–8 MINUTES

SERVES 4

INGREDIENTS

2 tbsp olive oil

3 tbsp tequila

3 tbsp freshly squeezed orange juice

1 tbsp freshly squeezed lime juice

3 garlic cloves, crushed

2 tsp chili powder

2 tsp ground cumin

1 tsp dried oregano

salt and pepper

4 sirloin steaks

Place the oil, tequila, orange and lime juices, garlic, chili powder, cumin, oregano, and salt and pepper to taste in a large, shallow, nonmetallic dish and mix together. Add the steaks and turn to coat in the marinade. Cover and let chill in the refrigerator for at least 2 hours or overnight, turning occasionally.

Preheat the barbecue and oil the grill rack. Let the steaks return to room temperature, then remove from the marinade. Cook over hot coals for 3–4 minutes on each side for medium, or longer according to taste, basting frequently with the marinade. Serve at once. Alternatively, cook the steaks under a preheated hot broiler.

MAIN COURSES

2 cups fresh ground lamb

1 small onion, finely chopped

1 tsp ground cumin

1 tsp ground coriander

1 tsp chili powder

1 tsp garam masala

1 tsp garlic paste

2 tbsp chopped fresh cilantro

salt

scant 1 cup vegetable oil

6 scallions, chopped

1 green bell pepper, seeded
and chopped

6 oz/175 g fava beans, thawed
if frozen

12 baby corn, thawed if frozen

1 small cauliflower, cut into florets

3 fresh green chilies, seeded
and chopped

1 tbsp lime juice

1 tbsp fresh mint leaves

PREPARE 20 MINUTES

COOK 25 MINUTES

SERVES 4

Place the lamb, onion, cumin, ground coriander, chili powder, garam masala, garlic paste, and half the fresh cilantro in a bowl and mix well with your hands. Season with salt to taste. Cover with plastic wrap and let chill in the refrigerator for a few minutes.

Heat 3 tablespoons of the vegetable oil in a preheated wok or large skillet. Add the scallions and cook, stirring frequently, for 1 minute. Add the green bell pepper, fava beans, corn, cauliflower, and chilies and cook over high heat, stirring, for 3 minutes, or until crisp-tender. Set aside.

Heat the remaining vegetable oil in a separate preheated wok or large skillet. Meanwhile, form the lamb mixture into small balls or ovals between the palms of your hands. Add the koftas, in batches, to the hot oil and cook, turning them frequently, until golden brown. Remove with a slotted spoon and drain on paper towels. When they are all cooked, return the vegetables to the heat, and stir in the koftas. Cook over low heat, stirring frequently, for 5 minutes, or until heated through. Sprinkle with the lime juice and serve garnished with the remaining cilantro and the mint leaves.

Lamb Koftas

Cod in Spicy Coconut Sauce

**PREPARE 15 MINUTES,
PLUS 30 MINUTES' SOAKING**

COOK 30 MINUTES

SERVES 4

INGREDIENTS

1 oz/25 g dried tamarind,
coarsely chopped

⅔ cup boiling water

4 tbsp ghee or vegetable oil

2 tsp mustard seeds

1 tsp fenugreek seeds

1 tsp ginger paste

2 fresh green chilies, seeded
and chopped

6 curry leaves

2 onions, chopped

1 tsp chili powder

1 tsp ground turmeric

1 tsp ground cumin

14 oz/400 g canned tomatoes, drained

generous 1¾ cups canned coconut milk

salt

4 cod fillets, skinned

3 tbsp chopped fresh cilantro

freshly cooked rice, to serve

lime slices, to garnish

Place the dried tamarind in a bowl and pour in the boiling water. Let soak for 30 minutes. Heat the ghee in a large, heavy-bottom pan. Add the mustard seeds and cook over a low heat, stirring constantly, for 2 minutes, or until they give off their aroma. Add the fenugreek seeds, ginger paste, chilies, and curry leaves and cook, stirring constantly, for 2 minutes, then add the onions. Cook, stirring occasionally, for 10 minutes, or until golden.

Stir in the chili powder, turmeric, cumin, and drained tomatoes and cook for 2–3 minutes, then add the coconut milk. Season with salt to taste and let simmer, stirring occasionally, for 5 minutes. Strain the tamarind into a clean bowl, pressing down on the pulp with the back of a wooden spoon. Discard the pulp and add the liquid to the pan with the fish.

Cover the pan and let simmer gently for 6–10 minutes, or until the fish is tender and cooked through. The flesh should flake easily when tested with the tip of a knife. Sprinkle with chopped cilantro and serve with rice, garnished with lime slices.

INGREDIENTS

1 lb 5 oz/600 g raw shrimp, shelled

2 tbsp chopped fresh flat-leaf parsley

12 tortilla shells

sour cream

chopped scallions, to garnish

corn and bell pepper salsa, to serve

TACO SAUCE

1 tbsp olive oil

1 onion, finely chopped

1 green bell pepper, cored, seeded
and diced

1–2 fresh hot green chilies, such
as jalapeño, seeded and finely chopped

3 garlic cloves, crushed

1 tsp ground cumin

1 tsp ground coriander

1 tsp brown sugar

1 lb/450 g ripe tomatoes, peeled
and coarsely chopped

juice of ½ lemon

salt and pepper

PREPARE 20 MINUTES

COOK 35 MINUTES

SERVES 4

Preheat the oven to 350°F/180°C. To make the sauce, heat the oil in a deep skillet over medium heat. Add the onion and cook for 5 minutes, or until softened. Add the bell pepper and chilies and cook for 5 minutes. Add the garlic, cumin, coriander, and sugar and cook the sauce for an additional 2 minutes, stirring.

Add the tomatoes, lemon juice, and salt and pepper to taste. Bring to a boil, then reduce the heat and let simmer for 10 minutes.

Stir in the shrimp and parsley, cover, and cook gently for 5–8 minutes until the shrimp are pink and tender.

Meanwhile, place the tortilla shells, open-side down, on a baking sheet. Warm in the oven for 2–3 minutes.

To serve, spoon the shrimp mixture into the tortilla shells, top with a spoonful of sour cream, and garnish with chopped scallions. Serve with a little corn and bell pepper salsa, if desired.

Chili-Shrimp Tacos

Vegetable Biryani

PREPARE 20 MINUTES
PLUS 5 MINUTES' STANDING

COOK 30 MINUTES

SERVES 4

INGREDIENTS

2 tbsp vegetable oil

3 whole cloves

3 cardamom pods, cracked

1 onion, chopped

4 oz/115 g carrots, chopped

2–3 garlic cloves, crushed

1–2 fresh red chilies, seeded and chopped

1-inch/2.5-cm piece fresh gingerroot, grated

4 oz/115 g cauliflower, broken into small florets

6 oz/175 g broccoli, broken into small florets

4 oz/115 g green beans, chopped

14 oz/400 g canned chopped tomatoes

⅔ cup vegetable stock

salt and pepper

4 oz/115 g okra, sliced

1 tbsp chopped fresh cilantro, plus extra sprigs to garnish

generous ¼ cup brown basmati rice

few saffron threads (optional)

zested lime rind, to garnish

Heat the oil in a large pan over low heat, add the spices, onion, carrots, garlic, chilies, and ginger and cook, stirring frequently, for 5 minutes.

Add all the vegetables, except the okra, and cook, stirring frequently, for 5 minutes. Stir in the tomatoes, stock, and salt and pepper to taste and bring to a boil. Reduce the heat, cover, and let simmer for 10 minutes.

Add the okra and cook for an additional 8–10 minutes, or until the vegetables are tender. Stir in the cilantro. Strain off any excess liquid and keep warm.

Meanwhile, cook the rice with the saffron in a pan of lightly salted boiling water for 25 minutes, or until tender. Drain and keep warm.

Layer the vegetables and cooked rice in a deep dish or ovenproof bowl, packing the layers down firmly. Let stand for about 5 minutes, then invert onto a warmed serving dish and serve, garnished with zested lime rind and cilantro sprigs, with the reserved liquid.

INGREDIENTS

generous ¾ cup each dried black beans, cannellini beans and pinto beans, soaked overnight in separate bowls in water to cover

2 tbsp olive oil

1 large onion, finely chopped

2 red bell peppers, seeded and diced

2 garlic cloves, very finely chopped

½ tsp cumin seeds, crushed

1 tsp coriander seeds, crushed

1 tsp dried oregano

½–2 tsp chili powder

3 tbsp tomato paste

1 lb 12 oz/800 g canned chopped tomatoes

1 tsp sugar

1 tsp salt

2½ cups vegetable stock

3 tbsp chopped fresh cilantro

PREPARE 20 MINUTES

COOK 1 HOUR 40 MINUTES – 2 HOURS

SERVES 6

Drain the beans, put in separate pans, and cover with cold water. Bring to a boil and boil vigorously for 10–15 minutes, then reduce the heat and let simmer for 35–45 minutes until just tender. Drain and set aside.

Heat the oil in a large, heavy-bottom pan over medium heat. Add the onion and bell peppers and cook, stirring frequently, for 5 minutes, or until softened.

Add the garlic, cumin, and coriander seeds and oregano and cook, stirring, for 30 seconds until the garlic is beginning to color. Add the chili powder and tomato paste and cook, stirring, for 1 minute. Add the tomatoes, sugar, salt, beans, and stock. Bring to a boil, then reduce the heat, cover, and let simmer, stirring occasionally, for 45 minutes.

Stir in the fresh cilantro. Ladle into individual warmed bowls and serve immediately.

Mexican Three-Bean Chili

Vegetable Korma

PREPARE 20 MINUTES

COOK 40 MINUTES

SERVES 4

INGREDIENTS

4 tbsp ghee or vegetable oil

2 onions, chopped

2 garlic cloves, chopped

1 fresh red chili, chopped

1 tbsp grated fresh gingerroot

2 tomatoes, peeled and chopped

1 orange bell pepper, seeded and cut
into small pieces

1 large potato, cut into chunks

7 oz/200 g cauliflower florets

½ tsp salt

1 tsp turmeric

1 tsp ground cumin

1 tsp ground coriander

1 tsp garam masala

scant 1 cup vegetable stock or water

⅔ cup plain yogurt

⅔ cup light cream

1 oz/25 g fresh cilantro, chopped

freshly cooked rice, to serve

Heat the ghee in a large pan over medium heat, add the onions and garlic, and cook, stirring frequently, for 3 minutes. Add the chili and ginger and cook for an additional 4 minutes. Add the tomatoes, orange bell pepper, potato, cauliflower, salt, and spices and cook, stirring constantly, for another 3 minutes. Stir in the stock and bring to a boil. Reduce the heat and simmer for 25 minutes.

Stir in the yogurt and cream and cook, stirring frequently, for an additional 5 minutes without boiling. Add the fresh cilantro and heat through.

Serve with freshly cooked rice.

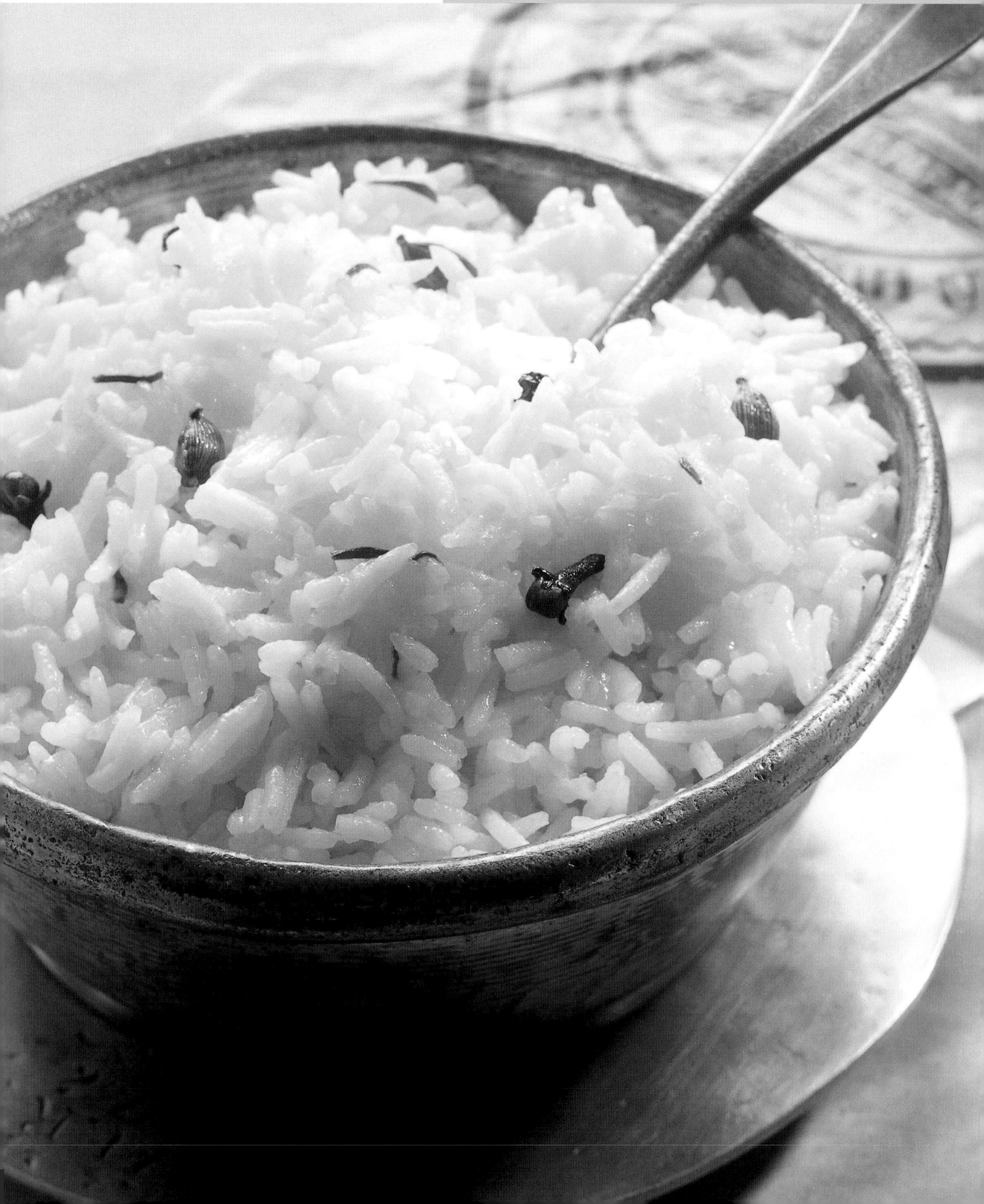

ACCOMPANIMENTS

Fabulous, spicy side dishes can make all the difference to a meal, turning a simple chop or basic poached fish into a new taste experience. Potatoes and rice need never be boring again, while everyone will relish the special flavors of the other vegetable dishes, such as Stir-fried Ginger Mushrooms (see page 64).

ACCOMPANIMENTS

INGREDIENTS

1 lb 8 oz/675 g large, firm potatoes, such as round white, round red, Yukon gold, or russet

3 tbsp vegetable oil

1 tbsp paprika or 2 tsp ground coriander

1 tsp cumin seeds

1 tsp turmeric

salt and pepper

chopped fresh cilantro, to garnish

PREPARE 10 MINUTES

COOK 40–45 MINUTES

SERVES 4

Preheat the oven to 400°F/200°C. Scrub the potatoes, then cut each in half lengthwise and then in half again until you have 8 even-shaped wedges. Put into a large pan of salted water, bring to a boil, and boil for 3 minutes. Drain well and return the wedges to the pan.

Add the oil to the pan and toss the potato wedges in it until coated. Add the paprika, cumin seeds, and turmeric, season to taste with salt and pepper, and mix well together.

Spread the potato wedges out on a baking sheet and bake in the oven for 35–40 minutes until tender and golden brown, turning 2–3 times during cooking. Serve hot, sprinkled with chopped cilantro to garnish.

54

Spicy Potato Wedges

Mixed Vegetables

PREPARE 15 MINUTES

COOK 45 MINUTES

SERVES 4

INGREDIENTS

1¼ cups vegetable oil

1 tsp mustard seeds

1 tsp onion seeds

½ tsp white cumin seeds

3–4 curry leaves, chopped

1 lb/450 g onions, finely chopped

3 tomatoes, chopped

½ red bell pepper, seeded and sliced

½ green bell pepper, seeded and sliced

1 tsp finely chopped fresh gingerroot

1 tsp crushed fresh garlic

1 tsp chili powder

¼ tsp ground turmeric

1 tsp salt

scant 2 cups water

2 potatoes, peeled and cut into pieces

½ cauliflower, cut into small florets

4 carrots, sliced

3 fresh green chilies, finely chopped

2–3 tbsp fresh cilantro leaves

1 tbsp lemon juice

freshly cooked rice, to serve

Heat the vegetable oil in a large, heavy-bottom pan. Add the mustard seeds, onion seeds, and white cumin seeds with the curry leaves and cook until they turn a darker color.

Add the onions to the pan and cook over medium heat for 8 minutes, until golden.

Add the tomatoes and bell peppers and stir-fry for 5 minutes. Add the ginger, garlic, chili powder, turmeric, and salt and mix well.

Add 1¼ cups of the water, cover, and let simmer for 10–12 minutes, stirring occasionally.

Add the potatoes, cauliflower, carrots, green chilies, and cilantro leaves and stir-fry for 5 minutes. Add the remaining water and lemon juice, and stir well. Cover and let simmer for 15 minutes, stirring occasionally. Transfer the mixed vegetables to serving plates and serve with rice.

ACCOMPANIMENTS

1 cup basmati rice

2 tbsp ghee

3 green cardamoms

2 whole cloves

3 black peppercorns

½ tsp salt

½ tsp saffron threads

1¾ cups water

Rinse the rice twice under cold running water and set aside.

Heat the ghee in a large, heavy-bottom pan. Add the cardamoms, cloves, and peppercorns and cook, stirring, for 1 minute. Add the rice and stir-fry for an additional 2 minutes.

Add the salt, saffron threads, and water to the rice mixture and reduce the heat. Cover the pan and let simmer over low heat for 20 minutes, or until all the water has evaporated.

Transfer the rice to a large, warmed serving dish and serve hot.

Pulao Rice

Deep-Fried Potato Balls

PREPARE 20 MINUTES

COOK 15 MINUTES

SERVES 4

INGREDIENTS

1 lb/450 g potatoes, boiled and diced

1 onion, chopped

1-inch/2.5-cm piece fresh gingerroot,
finely chopped

1 fresh green chili, seeded
and finely chopped

1 tbsp chopped fresh cilantro

1 tbsp lemon juice

2 tsp aamchoor (dried mango powder)

salt

vegetable oil, for deep-frying

chutney, to serve

BATTER

¾ cup gram flour

¼ tsp baking powder

¼ tsp chili powder

salt

about ⅔ cup water

To make the batter, sift the flour, baking powder, chili powder, and a pinch of salt into a bowl. Gradually, stir in enough cold water to make a smooth batter. Cover with plastic wrap and set aside.

Place the potatoes, onion, ginger, chili, cilantro, lemon juice, and aamchoor into a separate bowl and season with salt to taste. Mix together well with a wooden spoon, breaking up the potatoes. Break off small pieces of the mixture and form into balls between the palms of your hands.

Heat the vegetable oil in a deep-fat fryer or heavy-bottom pan to 350–375°F/180–190°C, or until a cube of bread browns in 30 seconds. When the oil is hot, dip the potato balls in the batter, using a fork, and add to the oil, in batches. Deep-fry for 3–4 minutes, until golden brown. Remove with a slotted spoon and drain on paper towels. Keep each batch warm while you cook the remainder. Serve hot, with chutney.

ACCOMPANIMENTS

1 lb 12 oz/800 g canned tomatoes

2 tbsp dry unsweetened coconut

2 tbsp lemon juice

1 tbsp yellow mustard seeds

scant ¼ cup raw or brown sugar

2 tbsp ghee or vegetable oil

2 onions, sliced

4 cardamom pods, lightly crushed

6 curry leaves, plus extra to garnish

2 tsp ground coriander

2 tsp ground cumin

1 tsp ground turmeric

1 tsp ginger paste

1 cup toor dal

1 lb/450 g sweet potatoes, cut
into chunks

2 lb/900 g potatoes, cut into chunks

2 carrots, sliced

2 zucchinis, cut into chunks

1 eggplant, cut into chunks

salt

PREPARE 25 MINUTES

COOK 55 MINUTES

SERVES 6

Place the tomatoes and their can juices, coconut, 1 tablespoon of the lemon juice, the mustard seeds, and sugar in a food processor or blender and process until smooth.

Heat the ghee in a large, heavy-bottom pan. Add the onion and cook over low heat, stirring occasionally, for 10 minutes, or until golden. Add the cardamoms, curry leaves, coriander, cumin, turmeric, and ginger paste and cook, stirring constantly, for 1–2 minutes, or until the spices give off their aroma. Stir in the tomato mixture and dal and bring to a boil. Reduce the heat, cover, and let simmer for 10 minutes.

Add the sweet potatoes, potatoes, and carrots, re-cover the pan, and let simmer for an additional 15 minutes. Add the zucchinis, eggplant, and remaining lemon juice, add salt to taste, re-cover, and let simmer for an additional 10–15 minutes, or until the vegetables are tender. Serve garnished with curry leaves.

Vegetable Samber

Stir Fried Ginger Mushrooms

PREPARE 15 MINUTES

COOK 10 MINUTES

SERVES 4

INGREDIENTS

2 tbsp vegetable oil

3 garlic cloves, crushed

1 tbsp Thai red curry paste

½ tsp ground turmeric

15 oz/425 g canned straw mushrooms,
drained and halved

¾-inch/2-cm piece fresh gingerroot,
finely shredded

scant ½ cup coconut milk

1½ oz/40 g dried shiitake mushrooms,
soaked, drained, and sliced

1 tbsp lemon juice

1 tbsp light soy sauce

2 tsp sugar

½ tsp salt

8 cherry tomatoes, halved

7 oz/200 g firm tofu
(drained weight), diced

cilantro leaves, for sprinkling

freshly cooked Thai fragrant rice, to serve

Heat the oil in a preheated wok or large skillet. Add the garlic and cook for 1 minute, stirring. Stir in the curry paste and turmeric and cook for an additional 30 seconds.

Stir in the straw mushrooms and ginger and stir-fry for 2 minutes. Stir in the coconut milk and bring to a boil.

Stir in the shiitake mushrooms, lemon juice, soy sauce, sugar, and salt and heat thoroughly. Add the tomatoes and tofu and toss gently to heat through.

Sprinkle the cilantro over the mixture and serve hot with freshly cooked fragrant rice.

INGREDIENTS

generous 1 cup basmati rice

2½ cups water

2 whole cloves

4 cardamom pods, lightly crushed

1 cinnamon stick

pinch of saffron threads, lightly crushed

salt

2 tbsp lime juice

1 tbsp finely grated lime rind

⅓ cup golden raisins

scant ½ cup pistachios, coarsely chopped

PREPARE 10 MINUTES,
PLUS 15 MINUTES' SOAKING/STANDING

COOK 20 MINUTES

SERVES 4

Rinse the rice in several changes of water and let soak for 10 minutes. Drain well.

Pour the water into a large, heavy-bottom pan, add the cloves, cardamoms, cinnamon stick, saffron threads, and a pinch of salt and bring to a boil over medium heat. Add the rice and return to a boil. Reduce the heat, cover tightly, and let simmer for 10–15 minutes. Remove the pan from the heat and let stand, still covered, for 5 minutes.

Uncover the rice and fluff up the grains with a fork, then gently stir in the lime juice, rind, golden raisins, and pistachios. Taste and adjust the seasoning, if necessary, and serve.

Rice with Warm Spices

Bombay Potatoes

PREPARE 10 MINUTES

COOK 30 MINUTES

SERVES 6

INGREDIENTS

1 lb 2 oz/500 g new potatoes, diced

1 tsp ground turmeric

salt

4 tbsp ghee or vegetable oil

6 curry leaves

1 dried red chili

2 fresh green chilies, chopped

½ tsp kalonji seeds

1 tsp mixed mustard and onion seeds

½ tsp cumin seeds

½ tsp fennel seeds

¼ tsp asafoetida

2 onions, chopped

5 tbsp chopped fresh cilantro

juice of ½ lime

Place the potatoes in a large, heavy-bottom pan and pour in just enough cold water to cover. Add ½ teaspoon of the turmeric and a pinch of salt and bring to a boil. Let simmer for 10 minutes, or until tender, then drain and set aside until required.

Heat the ghee in a large, heavy-bottom skillet. Add the curry leaves and dried red chili and cook, stirring frequently, for a few minutes, or until the chili is blackened. Add the remaining turmeric, the fresh chilies, the kalonji, mustard, onion, cumin and fennel seeds, and the asafoetida, onions, and fresh cilantro and cook, stirring constantly, for 5 minutes, or until the onions have softened.

Stir in the potatoes and cook over low heat, stirring frequently, for 10 minutes, or until heated through. Squeeze over the lime juice and serve.

ACCOMPANIMENTS

14 oz/400 g green beans

1 garlic clove, finely sliced

1 fresh red Thai chili, seeded and chopped

½ tsp paprika

1 lemongrass stem, finely chopped

2 tsp Thai fish sauce

½ cup coconut milk

1 tbsp corn oil

2 scallions, sliced

PREPARE 10 MINUTES

COOK 10 MINUTES

SERVES 4

Cut the beans into 2-inch/5-cm pieces and cook in boiling water for 2 minutes. Drain well.

Place the garlic, chili, paprika, lemongrass, fish sauce, and coconut milk in a food processor and process to a smooth paste.

Heat the oil in a large skillet or preheated wok. Add the scallions and stir-fry over high heat for 1 minute. Add the paste and bring the mixture to a boil.

Simmer for 3–4 minutes to reduce the liquid by about half. Add the beans and simmer for an additional 1–2 minutes, or until tender. Transfer to a serving dish and serve hot.

Red Bean Curry

DESSERTS & BEVERAGES

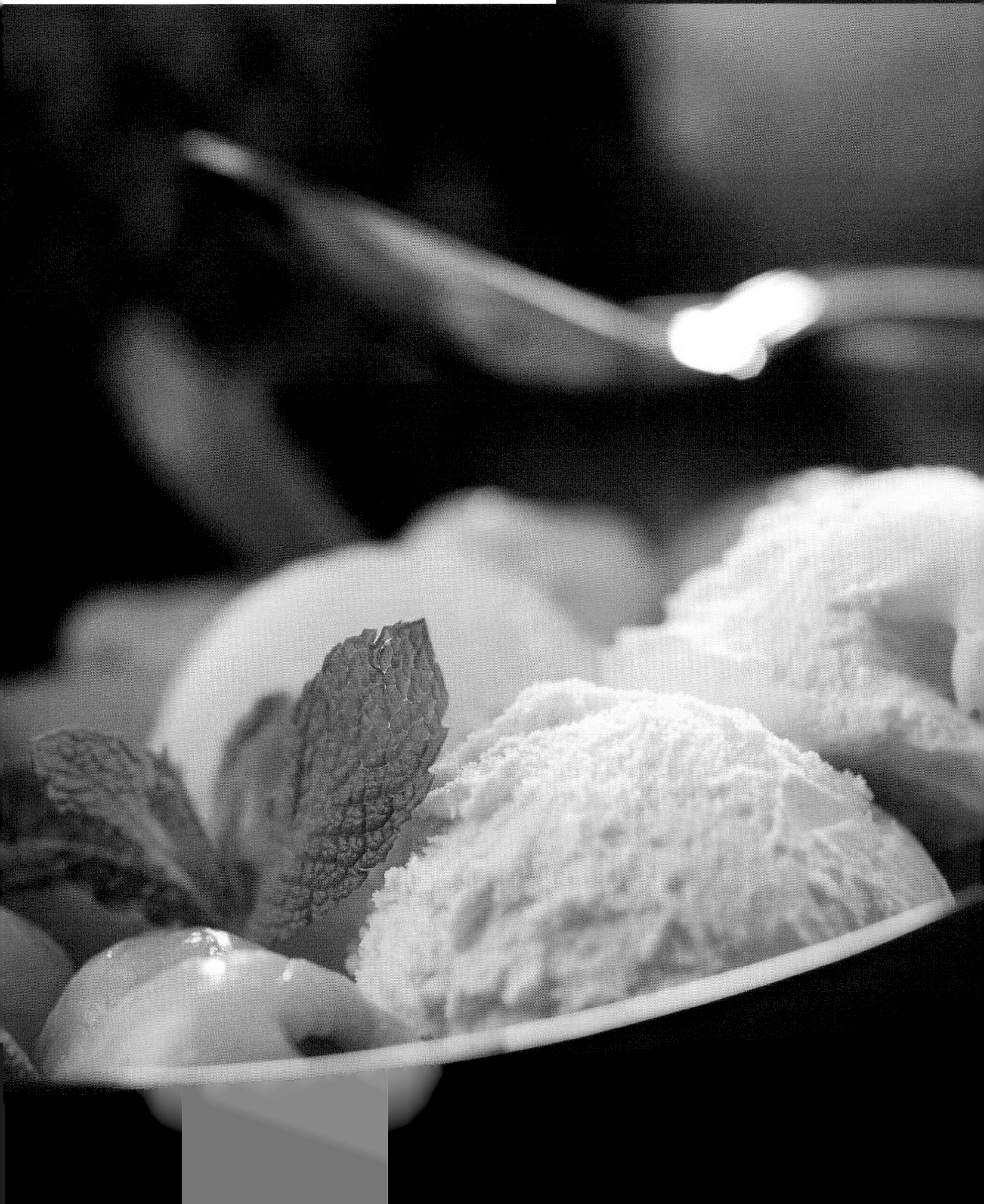

DESSERTS & BEVERAGES

Sweet dishes and drinks acquire a hint of adult sophistication when they are flavored with spices. Warm spices, such as cinnamon and ginger, are delicious additions to cakes, fruit, and even ice cream. Some unusual spicy additions enliven non-alcoholic drinks making them truly refreshing and a lovely surprise.

INGREDIENTS

4 eggs, plus 1 extra egg white

¼ tsp ground cinnamon

¼ tsp allspice

4 slices thick white bread

1 tbsp butter, melted

BERRIES

scant ½ cup superfine sugar

¼ cup freshly squeezed
orange juice

scant 2 cups mixed seasonal berries,
such as strawberries, raspberries,
and blueberries

PREPARE 10 MINUTES,
PLUS 10 MINUTES' COOLING

COOK 10 MINUTES

SERVES 4

Preheat the oven to 425°F/220°C. Place the eggs and egg white in a large shallow bowl and whisk together with a fork. Add the cinnamon and allspice and whisk until combined.

Soak the bread slices in the egg mixture for about 1 minute on each side. Brush a large baking sheet with the melted butter and place the bread slices on the sheet. Bake for 5–7 minutes, or until lightly browned. Turn the slices over and continue to bake for an additional 2–3 minutes.

Meanwhile, place the sugar and orange juice in a medium pan and bring to a boil over low heat, stirring to dissolve the sugar. Add the berries, turn off the heat, and let cool for 10 minutes. Serve spooned over the toast.

Spiced French Toast with Seasonal Berries

Simple Cinnamon Rolls

PREPARE 20 MINUTES,
PLUS 5 MINUTES' COOLING

COOK 35 MINUTES

MAKES 8 ROLLS

INGREDIENTS

scant 2½ cups self-rising flour

pinch of salt

2 tbsp superfine sugar

1 tsp ground cinnamon

3½ oz/100 g butter, melted, plus extra
for greasing

2 egg yolks

scant 1 cup milk, plus extra for glazing

FILLING

1 tsp ground cinnamon

generous ¼ cup brown sugar

2 tbsp superfine sugar

1 tbsp butter, melted

FROSTING

generous 1 cup confectioners'
sugar, sifted

2 tbsp cream cheese, softened

1 tbsp butter, softened

about 2 tbsp boiling water

1 tsp vanilla extract

Preheat the oven to 350°F/180°C. Grease an 8-inch/20-cm round pan and line the bottom with parchment paper.

Mix the flour, salt, superfine sugar, and cinnamon together in a bowl. Whisk the butter, egg yolks, and milk together and combine with the dry ingredients to make a soft dough. Turn out onto a large piece of waxed paper, lightly sprinkled with flour, and roll out to a rectangle 12 x 10 inches/ 30 x 25 cm.

To make the filling, mix the ingredients together, spread evenly over the dough and roll up, jelly-roll style, to form a log. Using a sharp knife, cut the dough into 8 even-size slices and pack into the prepared pan. Brush gently with extra milk and bake for 30–35 minutes, or until golden brown. Remove from the oven and let cool for 5 minutes before removing from the pan.

Sift the confectioners' sugar into a large bowl and make a well in the center. Place the cream cheese and butter in the center, pour over the water, and stir to mix. Add extra boiling water, a few drops at a time, until the frosting coats the back of a spoon. Stir in the vanilla extract. Drizzle over the rolls. Serve warm or cold.

1¾ cups coconut milk

1 cup whipping cream

4 egg yolks

5 tbsp superfine sugar

4 tbsp preserved ginger syrup

6 pieces preserved ginger, finely chopped

2 tbsp lime juice

fresh mint sprigs, to decorate

litchis

preserved ginger syrup, to serve

PREPARE 10 MINUTES,
PLUS 4½–6½ HOURS'
FREEZING/CHILLING

COOK 15 MINUTES

MAKES ABOUT 4 CUPS

Place the coconut milk and cream in a pan. Heat gently until just beginning to simmer. Remove the pan from the heat.

Beat the egg yolks, sugar, and ginger syrup together in a large bowl until pale and creamy. Slowly pour in the hot coconut milk mixture, stirring. Return to the pan and heat gently, stirring constantly, until the mixture thickens and coats the back of a spoon. Remove the pan from the heat and let cool. Stir in the ginger and lime juice.

Transfer the mixture to a large, freezerproof container. Cover and freeze for 2–3 hours, or until just frozen. Spoon into a bowl and mash with a fork or whisk to break down any ice crystals. Return the mixture to the container and freeze for an additional 2 hours. Mash once more, then freeze for 2–3 hours, or until firm.

Transfer to the refrigerator 20–30 minutes before serving. Decorate with mint sprigs and serve with litchis and a little ginger syrup drizzled over.

Coconut & Ginger Ice Cream

Walnut Cake

PREPARE 20 MINUTES,
PLUS 4 HOURS' COOLING

COOK 30 MINUTES

SERVES 12

INGREDIENTS

¾ cup plus 2 tbsp self-rising flour

½ tsp ground cinnamon

¼ tsp ground cloves

4 oz/115 g butter, softened

⅔ cup superfine sugar

4 eggs

1½ cups walnut pieces, chopped finely

pared rind and juice of 1 orange

⅔ cup white granulated sugar

2 tbsp brandy

Grease and line the bottom of a deep metal baking pan measuring 10 x 7 inches/25 x 18 cm with waxed paper.

Sift together the flour, cinnamon, and cloves. Put the butter and superfine sugar in a large bowl and beat together until light and fluffy. Add the eggs, one at a time, beating well after each addition. Using a metal spoon, fold in the sifted flour then fold in the walnuts.

Turn the mixture into the prepared pan and bake in a preheated oven, 375°F/190°C, for 30 minutes, until risen and firm to the touch.

Meanwhile, put the orange juice in a measuring cup and make up to ⅔ cup with water. Pour into a saucepan, add the granulated sugar and the pared orange rind, and heat gently until the sugar has dissolved. Bring to the boil and boil for 6 minutes until the mixture begins to thicken. Remove from the heat and stir in the brandy.

When the cake is cooked, prick the surface all over with a fine skewer then strain the hot syrup over the top of the cake. Leave in the pan for at least 4 hours before serving.

INGREDIENTS

8 crisp eating apples

1 tbsp lemon juice

½ cup golden raisins

1 tsp ground cinnamon

½ tsp grated nutmeg

1 tbsp brown sugar

6 sheets phyllo pastry

vegetable oil spray

confectioners' sugar,
to serve

CIDER SAUCE

1 tbsp cornstarch

2 cups cider

PREPARE 25 MINUTES

COOK 15–20 MINUTES

SERVES 2–4

Preheat the oven to 375°F/190°C. Line a baking sheet with nonstick paper. Peel and core the apples and chop them into $1/2$-inch/1-cm dice. Toss the pieces in a bowl, with the lemon juice, golden raisins, cinnamon, nutmeg, and sugar.

Lay out a sheet of phyllo pastry, spray with vegetable oil, and lay a second sheet on top. Repeat with a third sheet. Spread over half the apple mixture and roll up lengthwise, tucking in the ends to enclose the filling. Repeat to make a second strudel. Slide onto the baking sheet, spray with oil, and bake in the oven for 15–20 minutes.

For the sauce, blend the cornstarch in a pan with a little cider until smooth. Add the remaining cider and heat gently, stirring constantly, until the mixture boils and thickens. Serve the strudel warm or cold, dredged with confectioners' sugar and accompanied by the cider sauce.

Apple Strudel with Warm Cider Sauce

Ginger Chocolate Chip Squares

PREPARE 10 MINUTES

COOK 30 MINUTES

MAKES 15

INGREDIENTS

4 pieces preserved ginger in syrup

1½ cups all-purpose flour

1½ tsp ground ginger

1 tsp ground cinnamon

¼ tsp ground cloves

¼ tsp grated nutmeg

½ cup brown sugar

4 oz/115 g butter

⅓ cup corn syrup

½ cup semisweet chocolate chips

Preheat the oven to 300°F/150°C. Finely chop the preserved ginger. Sift the flour, ground ginger, cinnamon, cloves, and nutmeg into a large bowl. Stir in the chopped preserved ginger and sugar.

Put the butter and the syrup in a pan and heat gently until melted. Bring to a boil, then pour the mixture into the flour mixture, stirring all the time. Beat until the mixture is cool enough to handle.

Add the chocolate chips to the mixture. Press evenly into a 8 x 12-inch/20 x 30-cm jelly roll pan.

Bake in the oven for 30 minutes. Cut into squares, then let cool in the pan.

INGREDIENTS

1½ cups all-purpose flour, plus extra for dusting

1 tsp baking powder

¼ tsp salt

1 tbsp brown sugar

1 egg, beaten

2 tbsp butter, melted

about ½ cup evaporated milk

vegetable oil, for deep-frying

ORANGE-CINNAMON SYRUP

1½ cups water

grated rind of 1 small orange

4 tbsp freshly squeezed orange juice

½ cup brown sugar

1 tbsp honey

2 tsp ground cinnamon

PREPARE 20 MINUTES,
PLUS 30 MINUTES' RESTING

COOK 45 MINUTES

SERVES 4

Sift the flour, baking powder, and salt together into a large bowl. Stir in the sugar. Beat in the egg and butter with enough evaporated milk to form a soft, smooth dough.

Shape the dough into 8 balls. Cover and let rest for 30 minutes.

Meanwhile, to make the syrup, place the water, orange rind and juice, sugar, honey, and cinnamon in a heavy-bottom pan over medium heat. Bring to a boil, stirring constantly, then reduce the heat and let simmer gently for 20 minutes, or until thickened.

Flatten the dough balls to make cakes. Heat the oil for deep-frying in a deep-fryer or deep pan to 350–375°F/180–190°C, or until a cube of bread browns in 30 seconds. Deep-fry the bunuelos in batches for 4–5 minutes, turning once, or until golden brown and puffed. Remove with a slotted spoon and drain on paper towels. Serve with the syrup spooned over.

Bunuelos with Orange-Cinnamon Syrup

Christmas in Summer

PREPARE 5 MINUTES,
PLUS 1-2 HOURS' COOLING/
CHILLING

COOK 0 MINUTES

SERVES 2

INGREDIENTS

5 tbsp cranberry cordial

2 allspice berries, crushed

2 slices of orange

2 cinnamon sticks

generous 1 cup boiling water

2 scoops of luxury vanilla ice cream

Ensure that you use glasses that are suitable for holding boiling water.

Divide the cranberry cordial between the glasses, then add a crushed allspice berry, an orange slice, and a cinnamon stick to each glass.

Pour the boiling water into the glasses. Let cool, then let chill in the refrigerator.

When you are ready to serve, float a scoop of ice cream on the top of each glass.

1¾ cups water

4 cloves

1 small cinnamon stick

2 tea bags

3–4 tbsp lemon juice

1–2 tbsp brown sugar

slices of lemon, to decorate

Put the water, cloves, and cinnamon into a pan and bring to a boil. Remove from the heat and add the tea bags. Let infuse for 5 minutes, then remove the tea bags.

Stir in the lemon juice and sugar to taste. Return the pan to the heat and warm through gently.

Remove the pan from the heat and strain the tea into heatproof glasses. Decorate with slices of lemon and serve.

Spiced Lemon Tea

Sweet & Sour Lassi

PREPARE 5 MINUTES,
PLUS 35 MINUTES' CHILLING

COOK 0 MINUTES

SERVES 4

INGREDIENTS

about 10 saffron threads,
plus a few extra to decorate

1 tbsp boiling water

scant 2½ cups lowfat plain yogurt

1 cup ice water

2 tbsp superfine sugar

½ tsp ground cardamom

½ tsp ground cumin

crushed ice, to serve

Place the saffron in a small bowl and stir in the boiling water. Let stand for 5 minutes to infuse.

Pour the yogurt into a large bowl and whisk for 2 minutes, until frothy. Whisk in the ice water and sugar, then stir in the cardamom, cumin, and saffron with its soaking water. Pour into a pitcher, cover with plastic wrap, and let chill in the refrigerator for 30 minutes.

To serve, fill tall glasses with crushed ice, pour in the lassi and decorate with a few saffron threads.

scant 2½ cups milk

scant 2½ cups water

4 tsp Darjeeling tea leaves

¼ cup fresh mint leaves

1 tsp ground ginger

1 tsp cardamom pods, lightly crushed

1 tsp fennel seeds

½ tsp freshly grated nutmeg

2 cinnamon sticks

sugar, to serve (optional)

Pour the milk and water into a heavy-bottom pan and bring to a boil.

Meanwhile, mix the tea leaves, mint leaves, ginger, cardamoms, fennel seeds, nutmeg, and cinnamon sticks together in a teapot or heatproof pitcher.

As soon as it boils, pour the milk and water mixture into the teapot and stir well. Let brew for 4–5 minutes, then strain into cups and serve, sweetened with sugar, if you like.

Hot Spiced Tea

INDEX